MINDSET Matters

TEEN EDITION

A 90-DAY JOURNEY OF CONFIDENCE, PEACE & PURPOSE

DEDICATION

For Madison and Gabrielle

My daughters.
My heart.
My inspiration.
Watching you grow, learn, question, dream, and become
has shown me the true meaning of strength, courage, and
love.

Everything I create, I create with you in mind —
your future, your voice, your joy, your truth.
May you always know how powerful you are.
May you always trust your gifts.
May you always believe in the light inside you.
And may you grow into the fullest, brightest version of
yourselves with confidence, grace, and purpose.
This journal is a reflection of what I want most for you both:
peace in your minds, clarity in your hearts, and unwavering
belief in who you're becoming.

I love you endlessly, and I am proud of you more than words
can ever say.
— *Mom*

And to every teen learning how to understand their
thoughts, feel their feelings, and believe in who they are
becoming —

This journal is for you.

WELCOME LETTER

Hey friend,
Welcome to Mindset Matters: Teen Edition.
I'm so glad you're here.

These pages are your space — a safe place to breathe, think, express yourself, and grow. Life can feel confusing, overwhelming, or even a little blurry sometimes. School, family, friendships, emotions, expectations… it's a lot. But you know what? You're stronger than you think. You're growing every day, even on the days you don't feel it.

This journal is here to help you slow down, check in with yourself, and focus on what really matters: your mindset.
 Because when your mind is centered, calm, and confident, everything else becomes easier to handle.

Over the next 90 days, you'll learn how to:
✨ Build confidence
✨ Manage stress
✨ Focus your energy
✨ Speak kindly to yourself
✨ Dream boldly
✨ And grow into the person you're becoming
You don't need to be perfect.
You just need to be open.
Be honest. Be curious. Be yourself.
You're not doing this alone — I'm walking with you every step of the way.
Let's grow together.

With love and encouragement,
Dr. Shamarah J. Hutchins — TheMindologist

HOW TO USE THIS JOURNAL

This journal is simple, but powerful.
Every week follows the same rhythm:
Daily Flow → Weekly Reflection → Creative Prompt Moments → The Last Lap.

Here's how it works:
DAILY FLOW (Days 1–6)

Each day has five parts:
1. Mood Check
Your feelings matter.
Before you begin, take a moment to notice what's going on inside you.

2. Gratitude
Gratitude shifts your mind into a better place — instantly.

3. Affirmation of the Day
A powerful truth to repeat to yourself and reflect on.
Affirmations help shape your self-belief.

4. Reflection Coaching
This is where I talk to you.
I'll guide your thoughts, help you understand your emotions, and push you to grow.

5. **Daily Exercise**
Different every day — like:
- Mind Dump → Mind Shift
- Kindness Challenge
- Goal Mini-Steps
- Breathe + Reset
- Creative Spark

This keeps your journey fun and fresh!

HOW TO USE THIS JOURNAL (CONT'D)

WEEKLY REFLECTION (Day 7)

This page is your check-in with yourself.

You'll look at:
- ✔ What went well
- ✔ What challenged you
- ✔ What you learned
- ✔ How you cared for yourself
- ✔ What you want to grow in next

This is where you SEE your growth.

CREATIVE PROMPTS

Every few days, you'll get extra reflection challenges—fun, expressive pages that let you explore your identity, dreams, and feelings in new ways.

You can write, draw, sketch, brainstorm — whatever feels right.

The Last Lap (Days 85–90)

Your final week ties everything together.

You'll:
- ✦ Write a letter to your Day 1 self
- ✦ Record your gratitude
- ✦ Celebrate your wins
- ✦ Set your next vision
- ✦ Create your own personal affirmation
- ✦ Reflect on who you've become

You'll finish this book knowing yourself better — and believing in yourself more deeply.

HOW TO USE THIS JOURNAL (CONT'D)

WHAT IS MIND DUMP → MIND SHIFT EXPLAINED

Sometimes your mind gets crowded.
Thoughts pile up. Worries get heavy.
You start believing things that aren't even true.

That's where **Mind Dump → Mind Shift** comes in — it's your mental reset button.

Mind Dump:
Write down a negative thought or worry that's bothering you.
Get it out of your head and onto the page.
This frees your mind.

Mind Shift:
Now take that thought and flip it into truth.
Not fake positivity — honest, empowering truth.

"I can't do this" → "I can learn this one step at a time."
"No one cares about me" → "There ARE people who care about me."
"I'm failing" → "I'm learning and growing."

Mind Dump clears the clutter.
Mind Shift rewrites the story.

This tool will strengthen your mindset — every time you use it.

DAY 1

YOU ARE STRONGER THAN YOU THINK

Mood Check

Circle how you feel today.

One Word for Today

Write your word for today in the box.

Gratitude

Today I'm thankful for...

Affirmation of the Day

I AM STRONGER THAN MY CHALLENGES.

DAY 1
MINDSET COACHING

Today is the beginning of your journey.
And I want you to start with one truth: You are stronger than you think.
Even if you don't feel strong today. Even if life feels heavy. Even if you've been doubting yourself, you showed up. That is strength.

Challenges don't mean you're failing. They mean you're learning.
They mean you're growing.
They mean you're alive.

Let today be the day you stop underestimating yourself.
 You have more power than you realize — and over the next 90 days, you're going to prove it to yourself over and over again.

Reflection:
What challenge in your life can you face with strength today?

____

____

Daily Exercise – Mind Dump → Mind Shift
Write one negative or stressful thought:

____

Now rewrite it into something strong, true, and empowering:

____

____

____

DAY 2
FOCUS ON WHAT YOU CAN CONTROL

Mood Check

Circle how you feel today.

One Word for Today

Write your word for today in the box.

Gratitude

Today I'm thankful for...

DAY 2
MINDSET COACHING

Sometimes life feels overwhelming because you're trying to control things you can't — people's opinions, someone's mood, the past, the future, or circumstances outside your hands.

Today, I want you to shift your focus.
You have power — but not everywhere.
Your power lives in your choices, your reactions, your decisions, and your mindset.

When you stop trying to carry what isn't yours, you feel lighter.
When you focus on what is in your hands, you feel stronger.

Reflection:
What is one thing you can control today?

____

____

Daily Exercise – Gratitude 3
Write three things you're grateful for today:

1. ____

2. ____

3. ____

Circle the one that surprised you the most.

DAY 3

YOU ARE ENOUGH, EXACTLY AS YOU ARE

Mood Check

Circle how you feel today.

One Word for Today

Write your word for today in the box.

Gratitude

Today I'm thankful for...

Affirmation of the Day

I AM ENOUGH, JUST AS I AM.

DAY 3
MINDSET COACHING

You don't have to earn your worth.
You don't have to be perfect.
You don't have to have everything figured out.

You are already enough — right here, right now.

Maybe you've been comparing yourself to others.
Maybe you've been trying to prove something.
Maybe you've been feeling like you're "behind."

You're not behind.
You're becoming.
And who you are today is more than enough.

Reflection:
What makes me enough today?

____

____

Daily Exercise – Kindness Challenge
Do one kind thing today — for yourself or someone else.

Write it here: ____

How did it make you feel?

____

DAY 4

BELIEVE IN YOUR GROWTH

Mood Check

Circle how you feel today.

One Word for Today

Write your word for today in the box.

Gratitude

Today I'm thankful for...

Affirmation of the Day

I BELIEVE IN MY GROWTH.

DAY 4
MINDSET COACHING

Growth doesn't always feel like growth.
Sometimes it feels like confusion.
Or discomfort.
Or slow progress no one else can see.

But every time you choose to keep going — that's growth.
Every time you try again — that's growth.
Every time you learn something new — that's growth.

It's okay if you're not where you want to be yet.
What matters is that you are moving.

You are becoming someone stronger, wiser, and more confident every single day.

Reflection:
What is one way I'm growing right now?

____

____

Daily Exercise – Goal in Mini-Steps

Big Goal I want to work on _______________________________________

Step 1: _______________________________________

Step 2: _______________________________________

Step 3: _______________________________________

DAY 5

CREATE A PEACEFUL SPACE INSIDE YOURSELF

Mood Check

Circle how you feel today.

One Word for Today

Write your word for today in the box.

Gratitude
Today I'm thankful for...

DAY 5
MINDSET COACHING

You deserve peace.
Not just sometimes — every day.

Peace doesn't always come from outside you.
Sometimes you have to create it from the inside:
through breathing, pausing, setting boundaries, or choosing calm in moments that feel chaotic.

Today, let yourself slow down.
Let yourself breathe.
Let yourself feel safe inside yourself.

Reflection:
What helps me feel peaceful?

____

____

Daily Exercise – Breathe + Reset
Take 5 slow breaths.

Before breathing, I felt: _______________________________________

After breathing, I feel: ____

DAY 6

YOUR DREAMS ARE WORTH CHASING

Mood Check

Circle how you feel today.

One Word for Today

Write your word for today in the box.

Gratitude

Today I'm thankful for...

DAY 6
MINDSET COACHING

Today, I want you to think about your dreams — the big ones, the small ones, even the ones you're scared to say out loud.

Your dreams matter because you matter.
You don't have to have a perfect plan yet.
You just need the courage to believe that what you want is possible.

Every dream starts with a spark — a thought, a feeling, a "what if."
Let today be the day you honor that spark instead of ignoring it.
Trust that your dreams are leading you somewhere important. Trust that you deserve what you desire.

Reflection:
Which dream matters most to me right now?

____

____

Daily Exercise – Creative Spark
Draw or doodle something that represents your dream or how you feel today.

Label it with one meaningful word.
Word: _______________________________

WEEK 1 REFLECTION: LOOK AT YOUR GROWTH

Weekly Wins:
1. ____
2. ____

A Challenge I Faced:
____

What I Learned This Week:
____

How I Took Care of My Mindset:
____

One Way I Will Grow Next Week:
____

Creative Space:
Draw, sketch, write, or express something that represents your week.
This is your space — be real, be creative, be honest.

DAY 8

BE PROUD OF WHO YOU'RE BECOMING

Mood Check

Circle how you feel today.

One Word for Today

Write your word for today in the box.

Gratitude

Today I'm thankful for...

DAY 8
MINDSET COACHING

You are growing in ways you may not even see yet.
Sometimes growth is loud and exciting — but most of the time, it's quiet.
Invisible.
Happening underneath the surface.

The version of you you're becoming is stronger, wiser, calmer, and more confident.
Be proud of that.
Be proud of YOU.

Today is a good day to acknowledge the progress you've already made — not just in this journal, but in life.

Reflection:
What is one thing I'm proud of about myself right now?

____

____

Daily Exercise – Mind Dump → Mind Shift
Mind Dump (one negative thought):

____

Mind Shift (rewrite it into truth):

____

____

DAY 9

KINDNESS MAKES YOU POWERFUL

Mood Check

Circle how you feel today.

One Word for Today

Write your word for today in the box.

Gratitude

Today I'm thankful for...

I CHOOSE KINDNESS FOR MYSELF AND OTHERS.

DAY 9
MINDSET COACHING

Kindness isn't weakness.
It's strength — real strength.
It takes courage to be gentle in a world that can be rough.

And kindness isn't just for others — you need it too.
Talk to yourself gently.
Give yourself grace when you make mistakes.
Forgive yourself when you fall short.

Every time you choose kindness, you make the world a better place.
You also make your own world softer, warmer, and safer.

Reflection:
How can I show kindness today — to myself or someone else?

____

____

Daily Exercise – Gratitude 3
Write 3 things you're grateful for today:

1. _______________________________________

2. _______________________________________

3. _______________________________________

Circle the one that means the most today.

DAY 10

YOU'RE LEARNING EVERY DAY

Mood Check

Circle how you feel today.

One Word for Today

Write your word for today in the box.

Gratitude

Today I'm thankful for...

DAY 10
MINDSET COACHING

Life doesn't require you to know everything.
It asks you to learn, grow, and stay open.

Every mistake is a lesson.
Every challenge is a teacher.
Every emotion is a message.
Every experience shapes you into someone wiser.

Today, I want you to stop judging yourself for what you don't know yet — and start celebrating everything you're learning along the way.

You are a student of life, and you're doing better than you realize.

Reflection:
What is one lesson I've learned recently?

____

____

Daily Exercise – Act of Kindness Challenge
Do one kind thing today — big or small.

Write it here: _______________________________

How did it impact me (or someone else)?

____

____

____

DAY 11

YOU DESERVE TO TAKE UP SPACE

Mood Check

Circle how you feel today.

One Word for Today

Write your word for today in the box.

Gratitude

Today I'm thankful for...

DAY 11
MINDSET COACHING

Some days you might feel too quiet, too loud, too different, or like you don't fit in.

But hear me clearly:
You deserve to be here.
You deserve to be seen.
You deserve to take up space.

You don't have to shrink to make others comfortable.
You don't have to hide your voice, your personality, your opinions, or your dreams.

The world is big enough for your presence.
Your story.
Your light.

And the people who really matter?
They'll want you to stand tall — not small.

Reflection:
Where in my life do I need to show up more boldly?

Daily Exercise – Goal in Mini-Steps

Big goal I want to work toward: _______________________________________

Step 1: _______________________

Step 2: _______________________

Step 3: _______________________

DAY 12

RELEASE STRESS, WELCOME PEACE

Mood Check

Circle how you feel today.

One Word for Today

Write your word for today in the box.

Gratitude

Today I'm thankful for...

DAY 12
MINDSET COACHING

Your mind holds a lot — school, friendships, emotions, expectations, responsibilities.
Some of the stress you carry isn't even yours.

Today, I want you to gently let go.
Not of everything, but just one thing.
One thought.
One worry.
One pressure.

Peace doesn't show up by accident — you create it by giving yourself permission to rest.

You deserve that peace.
You deserve that breath.
You deserve that softness.

Reflection:
What stress can I release today to make room for peace?

____

____

Daily Exercise – Breathe + Reset
Take 5 slow breaths.

Before breathing, I felt: _______________________________________

After breathing, I feel: _______________________________________

Take 5 slow breaths. Let your shoulders drop. Let your mind settle.

____

____

DAY 13

TRUST YOURSELF MORE

Mood Check

Circle how you feel today.

One Word for Today

Write your word for today in the box.

Gratitude

Today I'm thankful for...

DAY 13
MINDSET COACHING

You've made it through every hard day of your life so far — which means you can trust yourself more than you give yourself credit for.

Trust your decisions.
Trust your intuition.
Trust your ability to handle things as they come.

You won't always know the perfect answer.
But you will figure things out as you go — because you always have.
Let today be a day where you listen to your inner voice instead of your doubts.

Reflection:
What decision do I need to trust myself with today?

____

____

Daily Exercise – Creative Spark
Draw or doodle something that symbolizes "trust" to you.

Add one word that matches the drawing.
Word: _______________________________________

WEEK 2 REFLECTION: CHECK YOUR PROGRESS

Weekly Wins:

   1. ____

   2. ____

A Challenge I Faced:

____

What I Learned This Week:

____

How I Took Care of My Mindset:

____

One Way I Will Grow Next Week:

____

Creative Space:
Draw, sketch, write, or express something that represents your week. This is your space — be real, be creative, be honest.

DAY 15

BE BRAVE ENOUGH TO BE YOURSELF

Mood Check

Circle how you feel today.

One Word for Today

Write your word for today in the box.

Gratitude

Today I'm thankful for...

Affirmation of the Day

I AM BRAVE ENOUGH TO BE MYSELF.

DAY 15
MINDSET COACHING

The bravest thing you can ever be in this world is yourself.
Not the version people expect.
Not the version you think others will like more.
Not the version that tries to fit in by shrinking.

YOU — exactly as you are — is powerful.
Being yourself takes courage.
It takes honesty.
It takes heart.

But nothing feels more freeing.
Nothing builds more confidence.
Nothing unlocks more joy.

Today, choose to show up as YOU — even if it feels scary.

Reflection:
Where in my life do I want to be more authentically myself?

____

____

Daily Exercise – Mind Dump → Mind Shift
Mind Dump (a fear or doubt about being yourself):

____

Mind Shift (the truth that replaces it):

____

____

DAY 16
NOTICE THE GOOD AROUND YOU

Mood Check

Circle how you feel today.

One Word for Today

Write your word for today in the box.

Gratitude
Today I'm thankful for...

DAY 16
MINDSET COACHING

It's easy to focus on what's going wrong — what feels stressful, messy, or uncertain.
But today, I want you to practice something powerful: noticing the good.

The good might be small — a smile from someone, something funny someone said, a cozy moment, fresh air, music you love, or a feeling you can't explain.

The good might be big — an accomplishment, a breakthrough, a moment of courage.

Either way, the more you look for good, the more your mind learns to see it.
Your brain is trainable.
Your attention is powerful.
What you focus on grows.

Reflection:
What is one good thing I noticed today (big or small)?

____

____

Daily Exercise – Gratitude 3
Write 3 things you're grateful for today:

1. ____

2. ____

3. ____

Circle the one that means the most today.

DAY 17

YOUR POSITIVITY CAN CHANGE A ROOM

Mood Check

Circle how you feel today.

One Word for Today

Write your word for today in the box.

Gratitude

Today I'm thankful for...

DAY 17
MINDSET COACHING

Your presence makes a difference.
When you walk into a room, you bring energy — and your energy matters.

Your smile, your attitude, your kindness, your vibe... these things impact people more than you realize.

You don't have to be loud.
You don't have to be perfect.
You don't have to be the most outgoing person.

Simply choosing to show up with a positive spirit can change someone's entire day — and it can shift your day too.

Today, think about how you want to show up.
How you want people to feel around you.How you want to feel inside yourself.

Reflection:
What's one way I can spread positivity today?

____

____

Daily Exercise – Act of Kindness
Do one kind thing today — big or small.

My act of kindness today: _______________________________

How it made me feel: _______________________________

DAY 18
CELEBRATE THE SMALL WINS

Mood Check

Circle how you feel today.

One Word for Today

Write your word for today in the box.

Gratitude
Today I'm thankful for...

DAY 18
MINDSET COACHING

Not every victory is big — and that's okay.
Small wins matter just as much.
They add up. They build confidence. They create momentum.

Small wins look like:
✦ getting out of bed even when you didn't want to
✦ turning in an assignment
✦ being kind to yourself
✦ showing up
✦ trying again
✦ asking for help
✦ choosing peace
✦ making progress

Success is built from tiny steps repeated over time.
Today, honor the little things.

Reflection:
What small win can I celebrate today?

____

____

Daily Exercise – Goal in Mini-Steps
Big goal I want to work toward: _________________________________

Step 1: _____________________

Step 2: _____________________

Step 3: _____________________

DAY 19

BREATHE OUT THE WORRY

Mood Check

Circle how you feel today.

One Word for Today

Write your word for today in the box.

Gratitude
Today I'm thankful for...

Affirmation of the Day

I BREATHE IN CALM AND EXHALE WORRY.

DAY 19
MINDSET COACHING

Worry tries to take over your mind — quietly at first, then loudly.
But your breath is stronger.
Your breath is a tool you carry with you everywhere.

When you breathe deeply, your mind slows down, your heart rate lowers,
and your body relaxes.
This isn't magic — it's biology.

Today, I want you to use your breath as your anchor.
When your thoughts race, slow them with steady breathing.
When your emotions spike, settle them with calm breaths.
When stress creeps in, breathe it out.

You're in control — one breath at a time.

Reflection:
What worry do I need to release today?

____

____

Daily Exercise – Breathe + Reset
Take 5 slow breaths.

Before breathing, I felt: _______________________________

After breathing, I feel: _______________________________

DAY 20

YOU ARE WORTHY OF LOVE AND RESPECT

Mood Check

Circle how you feel today.

One Word for Today

Write your word for today in the box.

Gratitude

Today I'm thankful for...

Affirmation of the Day

I AM WORTHY OF LOVE AND RESPECT.

DAY 20
MINDSET COACHING

You deserve love — real love.
Love from others, and love from yourself.
You deserve respect — from people around you, and from your own inner voice.

Sometimes you may forget this.
Sometimes you may let people treat you in ways you don't deserve.
Sometimes you may talk to yourself more harshly than you should.

Today is a reminder:
You are worthy.
Of softness.
Of kindness.
Of understanding.
Of respect.

Let this truth guide how you speak to yourself and how you allow others to speak to you.

Reflection:
What is one way I can show myself love or respect today?

____

____

Daily Exercise – Creative Spark
Draw or doodle something that symbolizes "trust" to you.

Add one word that matches the drawing.
Word: _________________________________

WEEK 3 REFLECTION: YOUR GROWTH IS SHOWING

Weekly Wins:
 1. ____
 2. ____

A Challenge I Faced:
____

What I Learned This Week:
____

How I Took Care of My Mindset:
____

One Way I Will Grow Next Week:
____

Creative Space:
Draw, sketch, write, or express something that represents your week. This is your space — be real, be creative, be honest.

DAY 22
PROGRESS OVER PERFECTION

Mood Check

Circle how you feel today.

One Word for Today

Write your word for today in the box.

Gratitude
Today I'm thankful for...

Affirmation of the Day

I FOCUS ON PROGRESS, NOT PERFECTION.

DAY 22
MINDSET COACHING

Perfection is a trap.
It tells you that you need to be "all the way there" before you can feel proud, confident, or successful.
But that's not true — progress is where growth lives.

Every step you take, every effort you make, every attempt you try — it all counts.
Your journey doesn't have to look flawless to be meaningful.

Today, give yourself permission to make mistakes, learn, try again, and grow at your own pace.
You're getting better every day — even when it feels slow.

Reflection:
What progress have I made recently, even if it feels small?

____

____

Daily Exercise – Mind Dump → Mind Shift
Mind Dump (a fear or doubt about being yourself):

____

Mind Shift (the truth that replaces it):

____

____

DAY 23

GRATITUDE MAKES YOU STRONGER

Mood Check

Circle how you feel today.

One Word for Today

Write your word for today in the box.

Gratitude

Today I'm thankful for...

DAY 23
MINDSET COACHING

Your journey isn't supposed to look like anyone else's.
You're learning lessons at your own pace.
You're discovering who you are, what you want, and what you value —
step by step.

Gratitude helps you see the beauty in your story instead of comparing it to someone else's.
It helps you appreciate what you have instead of focusing on what you don't.

Today, slow down and recognize the moments, memories, and people who have shaped you.
Your journey is one-of-a-kind — and that's a gift.

Reflection:
What part of my journey am I thankful for today?

____

____

Daily Exercise – Gratitude 3

1. ____

2. ____

3. ____

Circle the one that surprised you the most.

DAY 24

YOU CAN BE SOMEONE'S REASON TO SMILE

Mood Check

Circle how you feel today.

One Word for Today

Write your word for today in the box.

Gratitude
Today I'm thankful for...

DAY 24
MINDSET COACHING

It takes so little to brighten a day — a small compliment, a simple "thank you," one act of kindness, one moment of patience.

Kindness has a ripple effect.
When you lift someone else up, you lift yourself up too.
When you share positivity, it comes back to you in unexpected ways.

Today, choose to use your presence for good.
Not because you have to — but because you can.

There's something powerful about knowing your actions matter.

Reflection:
Who can I make smile today — and how?

____

____

Daily Exercise – Act of Kindness
Do one kind thing today — big or small.

My act of kindness today: _______________________________

How it made me feel: _________________________________

DAY 25
GROW IN THE DIRECTION OF YOUR GOALS

Mood Check

Circle how you feel today.

One Word for Today

Write your word for today in the box.

Gratitude
Today I'm thankful for...

DAY 25
MINDSET COACHING

Setting goals doesn't mean you must have everything figured out —
goals are simply a direction, a starting point, a promise to your future self.

You don't need perfect clarity.
You just need intention.

Every big dream begins with a small, brave step.
And every step forward, no matter its size, moves you closer to who you
want to be.

Today, take a moment to think about what matters to you.
What do you want to feel?
Who do you want to become?
What do you want to accomplish in the next few months?

Let your goals reflect your future — not your fears.

Reflection:
What goal feels important for me to focus on right now?

____

____

Daily Exercise – Goal in Mini-Steps

Big goal I want to work toward: _______________________________

Step 1: ______________________

Step 2: ______________________

Step 3: ______________________

DAY 26

RELEASE DISTRACTIONS, INVITE PEACE

Mood Check

Circle how you feel today.

One Word for Today

Write your word for today in the box.

Gratitude

Today I'm thankful for...

DAY 26
MINDSET COACHING

Distractions can pull your mind in a thousand directions — your phone, other people's drama, worried thoughts, social media, pressure, and expectations.

Not all distractions are bad… but some keep you from feeling peaceful, present, and connected to yourself.

Today, take a moment to notice what's pulling your attention away from what matters.
Then gently choose one distraction to release, even if just for the day.

Peace isn't found in a perfect environment.
Peace is created by choosing what to focus on — and what to let go.

Reflection:
What is one distraction I can let go of today so I can feel more peaceful?

____

____

Daily Exercise – Breathe + Reset
Take 5 slow breaths.

Before breathing, I felt: _______________________________

After breathing, I feel: _______________________________

Take 5 calm, slow breaths.

DAY 27
YOU'RE BUILDING YOUR FUTURE EVERY DAY
Mood Check

Circle how you feel today.

One Word for Today

Write your word for today in the box.

Gratitude
Today I'm thankful for...

DAY 27
MINDSET COACHING

Your future isn't something that suddenly appears one day — it's something you're building quietly, step by step, choice by choice.

Every decision you make — no matter how small — shapes who you're becoming.
Even the little things add up: your habits, your thoughts, your effort, your attitude, your courage, your curiosity.

You don't need to know every detail of your future.
You just need the desire to grow and the willingness to keep taking steps.
You're building something amazing — even on the days you can't see it yet.

Reflection:
What is one small thing I can do today for my future self?

____

____

Daily Exercise – Creative Spark
Draw or doodle something that represents the future you want.

Add one meaningful word.
Word: _______________________________________

WEEK 4 REFLECTION: RECOGNIZE YOUR WINS

Weekly Wins:
1. ____
2. ____

A Challenge I Faced:
____

What I Learned This Week:
____

How I Took Care of My Mindset:
____

One Way I Will Grow Next Week:
____

Creative Space:
Draw, sketch, write, or express something that represents your week. This is your space — be real, be creative, be honest.

DAY 29

YOU ARE CAPABLE OF LEARNING ANYTHING

Mood Check

Circle how you feel today.

One Word for Today

Write your word for today in the box.

Gratitude
Today I'm thankful for...

DAY 29
MINDSET COACHING

You were not born knowing everything — nobody is.
But you were born with the ability to learn, grow, and improve.

Every skill you admire in others?
They learned it.
Every talent someone has?
They practiced it.
Every success story you see?
It started with someone trying something new — just like you.

You are not "bad" at things.
You are learning.
And learning is powerful.

Today, don't be afraid of trying.
Don't be afraid of starting.
Don't be afraid of not knowing everything yet.

You're capable — far more capable than you realize.

Reflection:
What is one thing I want to learn or get better at right now?

____

____

Daily Exercise – Mind Dump → Mind Shift
Mind Dump: _______________________________________

Mind Shift: _______________________________________

DAY 30
GRATITUDE STRENGTHENS YOU

Mood Check

Circle how you feel today.

One Word for Today

Write your word for today in the box.

Gratitude
Today I'm thankful for...

DAY 30
MINDSET COACHING

Gratitude is one of the strongest tools you have.
It shifts your mindset from "what's missing" to "what's meaningful."
It helps your brain focus on the good instead of the stress.
It builds resilience — the strength to bounce back when life feels tough.
When you choose gratitude, you strengthen your heart, your mind, your peace, and your perspective.
Today, let yourself feel thankful — for moments, memories, people, lessons, or even your own progress.

Reflection:
How does gratitude make me stronger?

____

____

Daily Exercise – Gratitude 3

1. ____

2. ____

3. ____

Circle the one that surprised you the most.

DAY 31

SHINE YOUR LIGHT TODAY

Mood Check

Circle how you feel today.

One Word for Today

Write your word for today in the box.

Gratitude

Today I'm thankful for...

DAY 31

MINDSET COACHING

There is something special about you — something only you bring to the world.
Your humor, your creativity, your ideas, your energy, your heart.

These things are your light.
And when you hide your light, the world misses out.

Today, let yourself shine — not by being perfect or by impressing others, but by being authentically you.

Your light can brighten someone's day.
It can inspire.
It can comfort.
It can connect.
It can open doors — for you and for others.

Don't dim your shine.
Let it glow.

Reflection:
What is one way I can shine my light today?

____

____

Daily Exercise – Act of Kindness
Do one kind thing today — big or small.

My act of kindness today: ________________________________

How it made me feel: ___________________________________

DAY 32

BUILD THE HABITS THAT BUILD YOU

Mood Check

Circle how you feel today.

One Word for Today

Write your word for today in the box.

Gratitude

Today I'm thankful for...

DAY 32
MINDSET COACHING

Your habits shape your future — even the tiny ones.
Every small choice you make becomes part of who you're becoming.

Good habits don't require perfection.
They require consistency.
They require intention.
They require patience.

Think about the version of you you're growing into.
What do they do daily?
How do they treat themselves?
How do they show up?

Today, choose one small habit to strengthen.
One habit can change the direction of your whole week — even your whole life.

Reflection:
What is one habit I want to build or improve?

____

____

Daily Exercise – Goal in Mini-Steps

Habit I want to build: ___________________________________

Step 1: ______________________

Step 2: ______________________

Step 3: ______________________

DAY 33

LET GO OF WHAT YOU CAN'T CONTROL

Mood Check

Circle how you feel today.

One Word for Today

Write your word for today in the box.

Gratitude

Today I'm thankful for...

DAY 33
MINDSET COACHING

Holding on to things you can't control drains your energy — your peace, your joy, your mental space.

You can't control how others act.
You can't control what people think or say.
You can't control the past.
You can't control the future.

But you can control your choices.
Your reactions.
Your boundaries.
Your mindset.
Your effort.

Let go of what's not yours to carry.
Focus your energy on what's within your reach.

You'll feel lighter.
You'll think clearer.
You'll breathe easier.

Reflection:
What do I need to let go of today?

____

____

Daily Exercise – Breathe + Reset
Take 5 slow breaths.

Before breathing, I felt: _______________________________________

After breathing, I feel: _______________________________________

DAY 34
FOCUS HELPS YOU FLOURISH

Mood Check

Circle how you feel today.

One Word for Today

Write your word for today in the box.

Gratitude
Today I'm thankful for...

DAY 34
MINDSET COACHING

Your mind is powerful — but it can also get pulled in many directions.
Distractions, doubts, phones, people, stress...
If you don't choose your focus, something else will choose it for you.

Today, bring your attention back to what matters most.
Just because your mind wanders doesn't mean you're unfocused —it means you're human.
What matters is redirecting gently.

When you focus, you flourish.
You make progress.
You feel clearer.
You feel more confident.

Give your energy to what supports your growth — not what drains it.

Reflection:
What deserves my focus today?

____

____

Daily Exercise – Creative Spark
Draw or doodle something that represents the future you want.

Add one meaningful word.
Word: _______________________________

WEEK 5 REFLECTION: CELEBRATE YOUR PROGRESS

Weekly Wins:

   1. ____

   2. ____

A Challenge I Faced:

____

What I Learned This Week:

____

How I Took Care of My Mindset:

____

One Way I Will Grow Next Week:

____

Creative Space:
Draw, sketch, write, or express something that represents your week.
This is your space — be real, be creative, be honest.

DAY 36
YOU DON'T HAVE TO BE PERFECT TO BE VALUABLE

Mood Check

Circle how you feel today.

One Word for Today

Write your word for today in the box.

Gratitude
Today I'm thankful for...

DAY 36
MINDSET COACHING

Perfection is one of the biggest lies we tell ourselves.
You do not need to be perfect to deserve love, respect, opportunities, or confidence.

You don't need perfect grades.
You don't need a perfect mood.
You don't need a perfect body, friendship, performance, or life.

Your value comes from who you are — not what you perfect.

Today, I want you to breathe and give yourself permission to be human.
To try.
To learn.
To show up imperfectly and still be proud.

Reflection:
Where have I been too hard on myself lately?

____

____

Daily Exercise – Mind Dump → Mind Shift
Mind Dump (one belief about "not being enough"):

____

Mind Shift (the truth about my worth):

____

____

DAY 37
CHOOSE GRATITUDE, CHOOSE JOY

Mood Check

Circle how you feel today.

One Word for Today

Write your word for today in the box.

Gratitude
Today I'm thankful for...

DAY 37
MINDSET COACHING

Joy doesn't always show up on its own — sometimes you have to create it.
And one of the strongest ways to create joy is through gratitude.

When you focus on what's wrong, life feels heavy.
But when you focus on what's right — even the tiny things — your heart gets lighter.

Gratitude reminds you that good still exists.
That hope still exists.
That beauty still exists.
Even on hard days.

Today, choose gratitude like a mindset tool — not because everything is perfect, but because you deserve peace.

Reflection:
What am I genuinely grateful for today?

____

____

Daily Exercise – Gratitude 3

1. ____

2. ____

3. ____

Circle the one that means the most today.

DAY 38
YOUR WORDS HAVE POWER

Mood Check

Circle how you feel today.

One Word for Today

Write your word for today in the box.

Gratitude
Today I'm thankful for...

Affirmation of the Day
MY WORDS BRING LIFE AND POSITIVITY.

DAY 38
MINDSET COACHING

Words can build people up or break them down — including yourself. The way you speak to yourself matters.
The things you tell yourself shape your confidence, your mood, your choices, and your future.

So speak life into yourself:
 "I can do this."
 "I am getting better."
 "I matter."
 "I am enough."
 "I am growing."

And speak life into others too — it might mean more to them than you will ever know.

Today, pay attention to the words you use.
Make them powerful.
Make them uplifting.
Make them yours.

Reflection:
What positive words do I need to hear today — from myself?

____

____

Daily Exercise – Act of Kindness
Encourage someone today — with a text, a compliment, or a kind gesture.

What I did: ____

How it felt: ____

DAY 39
SMALL STEPS MAKE BIG DREAMS POSSIBLE

Mood Check

Circle how you feel today.

One Word for Today

Write your word for today in the box.

Gratitude
Today I'm thankful for...

DAY 39
MINDSET COACHING

Dreams don't happen all at once — they grow through small, consistent steps.
Every time you practice something, you grow.
Every time you try again, you grow.
Every time you work on a goal, even a tiny bit, you grow.

You don't need to have everything figured out.
You don't need the whole staircase — just the next step.

Today, focus on one small, simple action that moves you a little closer to who you want to become.
It counts. It matters. It builds momentum.

Reflection:
What small step can I take today for my dream?

____

____

Daily Exercise – Goal in Mini-Steps

Dream I want to work on: _______________________________

Step 1: _____________________

Step 2: _____________________

Step 3: _____________________

DAY 40
REST, RESET, AND REALIGN

Mood Check

Circle how you feel today.

One Word for Today

Write your word for today in the box.

Gratitude
Today I'm thankful for...

I ALLOW MYSELF TO REST AND REALIGN.

DAY 40
MINDSET COACHING

Sometimes the most powerful thing you can do is pause.
You've been showing up, thinking, growing—and that takes energy.

Rest is not quitting. Reset is not failure. Realigning is how you come back stronger and clearer.

When you give yourself space to breathe, you give yourself space to think, feel, and move with intention.

Today, let yourself slow down and check in.
You don't need to rush. You don't need to push.
You just need to realign.

Reflection:
What feels out of alignment in my life right now—and what do I need to reset?

____

____

Daily Exercise – Breathe + Reset
Take 5 slow breaths.

Before breathing, I felt: _______________________________

After breathing, I feel: _______________________________

DAY 41
YOUR POTENTIAL HAS NO LIMITS

Mood Check

Circle how you feel today.

One Word for Today

Write your word for today in the box.

Gratitude
Today I'm thankful for...

DAY 41
MINDSET COACHING

You are still growing, still learning, still evolving — and there is so much ahead of you.

Your dreams may be big, but so is your ability to reach them.
Never let anyone, including yourself, convince you that you're "not enough" or "too far behind."

You are limitless because you can learn new skills.
You can change your habits.
You can change your mindset.
You can create new opportunities.

Remember: your current situation is not your final destination.

Reflection:
Where in my life can I see my potential growing?

____

____

Daily Exercise – Creative Spark
Draw a symbol that represents "limitless" to you.

Label it with one powerful word:
Word: _______________________________________

WEEK 6 REFLECTION: LOOK BACK TO UNDERSTAND FORWARD

Weekly Wins:
1. ____
2. ____

A Challenge I Faced:
____

What I Learned This Week:
____

How I Took Care of Myself/Mindset:
____

One Way I Plan Grow Next Week:
____

Creative Space:
Draw, sketch, write, or express something that represents your week. This is your space — be real, be creative, be honest.

DAY 43

RELEASE WHAT WEIGHS YOU DOWN

Mood Check

Circle how you feel today.

One Word for Today

Write your word for today in the box.

Gratitude

Today I'm thankful for...

DAY 43
MINDSET COACHING

Sometimes your mind holds onto thoughts that aren't helping you —
fears, what-ifs, feelings of not being good enough, old conversations,
imaginary scenarios.

Carrying all of that gets heavy.
But you can choose to set it down.

You don't have to solve everything today.
You don't have to feel happy every moment.
You just need to make space for peace.

Today, let go of one negative thought.
Not because you're ignoring your feelings, but because you deserve
freedom.

Reflection:
What negative thought or emotion am I ready to release today?

____

____

Daily Exercise – Mind Dump → Mind Shift
Mind Dump: ____

Mind Shift: ____

DAY 44
GRATITUDE BRINGS YOU BACK TO CENTER

Mood Check

Circle how you feel today.

One Word for Today

Write your word for today in the box.

Gratitude
Today I'm thankful for...

DAY 44
MINDSET COACHING

When life feels overwhelming, gratitude brings you back to calm.
It reminds you that even in the chaos, there is still good.
Even in the stress, there is still beauty.
Even in the heaviness, there is still hope.

Today, slow down and notice one moment, one memory, or one person who brings warmth to your life.
Let that feeling ground you.

You are surrounded by more good than you realize.

Reflection:
Who or what am I most grateful for today — and why?

____

____

Daily Exercise – Gratitude 3

1. ____

2. ____

3. ____

Circle the one that means the most today.

✨ **Creative Reflection Prompt:**

Write a short thank-you note to someone who matters to you.
(It can be someone you know, or even yourself.)

____

____

DAY 45

KINDNESS IS YOUR SECRET SUPERPOWER

Mood Check

Circle how you feel today.

One Word for Today

Write your word for today in the box.

Gratitude

Today I'm thankful for...

DAY 45

MINDSET COACHING

Kindness is powerful.
 It can soften someone's bad day.
 It can strengthen friendships.
 It can heal hurt feelings.
 It can turn strangers into supporters.
 It can change your entire mood.

When you choose kindness, you choose courage, self-control, compassion, and strength.
And the world needs more of that — more of *you*.

Never underestimate the impact of one good deed, one gentle word, one positive choice.

Reflection:
How can I use my kindness to make a difference today?

____

____

Daily Exercise – Act of Kindness

Act of kindness I'll do today: _____________________________

How it made me feel: ____________________________________

DAY 46
PLAN YOUR DREAMS WITH CLARITY AND CALM

Mood Check

Circle how you feel today.

One Word for Today

Write your word for today in the box.

Gratitude
Today I'm thankful for...

DAY 46
MINDSET COACHING

It's okay not to know everything about your future.
You don't need the whole picture — you just need a direction.
Planning is not about pressure; it's about peace.
It's about giving your dreams space to breathe.
It's about getting clear on what matters to you.

Today, think about your dreams calmly.
No rushing.
No comparing.
No stressing.

Just you, your heart, and where you want to grow next.

Reflection:
What dream do I want to think about or plan for today?

____

____

Daily Exercise – Goal in Mini-Steps

Big goal I want to for: _______________________________

Step 1: ______________________

Step 2: ______________________

Step 3: ______________________

DAY 47
YOUR BREATH IS YOUR CALM SUPERPOWER

Mood Check

Circle how you feel today.

One Word for Today

Write your word for today in the box.

Gratitude
Today I'm thankful for...

DAY 47
MINDSET COACHING

Stress shows up in your body — in your shoulders, your stomach, your thoughts, your heartbeat.
But your breath can bring everything back into balance.

Breathing is your built-in tool.
You carry it everywhere.
It's always accessible.
It's always ready to help you slow down.

Today, use your breath to check in with your body.
Let it soften your stress.
Let it settle your thoughts.
Let it calm your spirit.

You deserve calm.

Reflection:
Where do I feel stress in my body right now?

____

____

Daily Exercise – Breathe + Reset
Take 5 slow breaths.

Before breathing, I felt: _______________________________

After breathing, I feel: _______________________________

DAY 48
FIND JOY IN THE LITTLE THINGS

Mood Check

Circle how you feel today.

One Word for Today

Write your word for today in the box.

Gratitude
Today I'm thankful for...

Affirmation of the Day
I CHOOSE JOY TODAY.

DAY 48
MINDSET COACHING

Some days joy comes easily.
Other days, you have to look for it — and that's okay.

Joy lives in little moments:
A favorite snack, a funny video, music that hits deep, laughing with
someone you care about, a quiet moment alone, sunlight through a window.

Today, look for the small things that make you smile.
Joy doesn't need to be loud to be powerful — it just needs to be felt.

Reflection:
What brought me joy today (even something tiny)?

____

____

Daily Exercise – Creative Spark
Draw or doodle something that made you smile today.

✨ **Creative Reflection Prompt:**
Make a joy list:
Write 3 things that always make you smile or laugh.

1. ____

2. ____

3. ____

WEEK 7 REFLECTION: STAY CONNECTED TO YOUR JOURNEY

Weekly Wins:

1. ____
2. ____

A Challenge I Faced:

____

What I Learned This Week:

____

How I Took Care of My Mindset:

____

One Way I Will Grow Next Week:

____

Creative Space:
Draw, sketch, write, or express something that represents your week.
This is your space — be real, be creative, be honest.

DAY 50
YOU HANDLE STRESS BETTER THAN YOU THINK

Mood Check

Circle how you feel today.

One Word for Today

Write your word for today in the box.

Gratitude
Today I'm thankful for...

DAY 50
MINDSET COACHING

Stress isn't the enemy — it's a signal.
It tells you where you need support, rest, boundaries, or clarity.

You've already survived things that once felt impossible.
You've handled more than you give yourself credit for.
You are stronger than your stress.

Today, instead of fighting stress, try understanding it.
What does it want you to pay attention to?
What needs to change?
What needs a pause?
What needs your calm?

Reflection:
What is one stress I can handle in a healthy way today?

____

____

Daily Exercise – Mind Dump → Mind Shift
Mind Dump (stressful thought):

____

Mind Shift (my empowering truth):

____

____

DAY 51
THERE IS BEAUTY IN SMALL MOMENTS

Mood Check

Circle how you feel today.

One Word for Today

Write your word for today in the box.

Gratitude
Today I'm thankful for...

Affirmation of the Day
I FIND BEAUTY IN LITTLE THINGS.

DAY 51
MINDSET COACHING

Life isn't only made up of big events — it's made of tiny moments that add warmth, joy, comfort, and meaning to your days.

A good meal.
A peaceful moment alone.
A song that hits your spirit.
A joke that makes you laugh.
A quiet breath of fresh air.
A hug.
A win that only you noticed.

Today, slow down enough to notice something small and good.
Beauty is always around you when you take time to see it.

Reflection:
What small moment felt beautiful to me today?

____

____

Daily Exercise – Gratitude 3
Write 3 things you're grateful for today:

1. _______________________________________

2. _______________________________________

3. _______________________________________

Circle the one that means the most today.

DAY 52
ENCOURAGE YOURSELF FOR TOMORROW

Mood Check

Circle how you feel today.

One Word for Today

Write your word for today in the box.

Gratitude
Today I'm thankful for...

Affirmation of the Day

I SPEAK TO MYSELF WITH ENCOURAGEMENT.

DAY 52
MINDSET COACHING

You talk to yourself more than anyone else... so your words matter.

Are you kind to yourself?
Do you hype yourself up?
Do you believe in your potential?
Do you remind yourself that you're capable, growing, and worthy?

You deserve encouragement — not just from others, but from yourself.

Today, practice speaking to yourself like you would to a friend:
kindly, patiently, and with love.

Reflection:
What encouraging message do I need to hear today?

____

____

Daily Exercise – Act of Kindness (Toward Self)
One kind thing I did for myself today: ____________________

How it felt: ____________________________________

✨ **Creative Reflection Prompt:**
Write a short pep talk to yourself for tomorrow.

____

____

____

DAY 53
FOCUS ON WHAT REALLY MATTERS TO YOU

Mood Check

Circle how you feel today.

One Word for Today

Write your word for today in the box.

Gratitude
Today I'm thankful for...

DAY 53
MINDSET COACHING

It's easy to get caught up in distractions — what other people think, what they're doing, how they're living.

But your life is your own.
Your path is your own.
Your focus is your superpower.

What truly matters to you?
Your peace?
Your goals?
Your family?
Your future?
Your happiness?

When you focus on what truly matters, everything else becomes noise.

Today, choose one thing that deserves your attention — and give it the best of you.

Reflection:
What matters most to me today — right now?

____

____

Daily Exercise – Goal in Mini-Steps
Big goal or priority: _________________________________

Step 1: _________________________________
Step 2: _________________________________
Step 3: _________________________________

DAY 54
RELAX YOUR MIND AND BODY

Mood Check

Circle how you feel today.

One Word for Today

Write your word for today in the box.

Gratitude
Today I'm thankful for...

DAY 55
MINDSET COACHING

When your mind is calm, everything becomes clearer.
Your thoughts make more sense.
Your emotions feel easier to understand.
Your decisions come from clarity, not panic.

Calm doesn't mean the world around you is quiet — it means *you* know how to stay steady inside yourself.

Today, trust your calm.
Trust that when you slow down, you can listen to your inner wisdom.
Trust that you don't need to rush.
You just need to breathe, think, and respond from a grounded place.

Reflection:
What decision can I make with more calm today?

____

____

Daily Exercise – Creative Spark
Draw or design something that represents "calm" to you — a wave, a cloud, a symbol, anything.

WEEK 8 REFLECTION: NOTICE YOUR INNER GROWTH

Weekly Wins:

1. ____
2. ____

A Challenge I Faced:

____

What I Learned This Week:

____

How I Took Care of My Mindset:

____

One Way I Will Grow Next Week:

____

Creative Space:
Draw, sketch, write, or express something that represents your week.
This is your space — be real, be creative, be honest.

DAY 57
YOU DON'T NEED TO HAVE ALL THE ANSWERS TODAY

Mood Check

Circle how you feel today.

One Word for Today

Write your word for today in the box.

Gratitude
Today I'm thankful for...

DAY 57
MINDSET COACHING

Growing doesn't mean knowing everything.
It means learning, exploring, trying, failing, trying again, and taking things one day at a time.

You are still discovering who you are.
Still figuring out what you want.
Still learning how to navigate life.

And that's exactly how it's supposed to be.

Release the pressure to have a perfect plan or perfect answers.
Your journey is unfolding at the pace meant for you.

Today, remind yourself that uncertainty isn't failure — it's the space where growth happens.

Reflection:
What is one thing I've been pressuring myself to figure out too fast?

____

____

Daily Exercise – Mind Dump → Mind Shift

Mind Dump:______________________________________

Mind Shift: ______________________________________

DAY 58
YOUR LESSONS MAKE YOU WISER

Mood Check

Circle how you feel today.

One Word for Today

Write your word for today in the box.

Gratitude
Today I'm thankful for...

DAY 58
MINDSET COACHING

Every experience — good or bad — teaches you something.
Every challenge shapes you.
Every mistake grows you.
Every emotion guides you.

You are becoming wiser, stronger, and more self-aware every single
day — even if it doesn't feel like it in the moment.

Today, honor the lessons life has given you.
Even the hard ones.
Even the unexpected ones.

They are shaping the version of you you're becoming.

Reflection:
What lesson have I learned recently that I'm grateful for?

____

____

Daily Exercise – Gratitude 3
Write 3 things you're grateful for today:

1. ____

2. ____

3. ____

Circle the one that means the most today.

DAY 59
YOUR PEACE MATTERS MORE THAN YOU REALIZE

Mood Check

Circle how you feel today.

One Word for Today

Write your word for today in the box.

Gratitude
Today I'm thankful for...

DAY 59
MINDSET COACHING

Your peace is precious.
It's what keeps you grounded, calm, clear, and emotionally healthy.
When you protect your peace, you protect your entire well-being.
You think better.
You feel better.
You respond better.
You grow better.

Protecting your peace might look like:
✨ Saying no
✨ Walking away from negativity
✨ Setting boundaries
✨ Taking a break
✨ Saying less
✨ Choosing quiet over chaos

Today, choose ONE thing you can do to safeguard your peace —
your spirit will thank you.

Reflection:
How can I protect my peace today?

____

____

Daily Exercise – Act of Kindness

What peaceful, kind action will I take today?:

____

How it made me feel:

____

DAY 60
STAY COMMITTED TO YOUR GROWTH

Mood Check

Circle how you feel today.

One Word for Today

Write your word for today in the box.

Gratitude
Today I'm thankful for...

DAY 60
MINDSET COACHING

Consistency is powerful — even if the steps feel small.
When you stay committed to your growth, you build a stronger, wiser
version of yourself day by day.

Consistency doesn't mean perfection.
It means showing up more days than you don't.
Trying again.
Choosing your growth even on slow days.
Recognizing that you're worth the effort.

Today, focus on one area of your life where you want to build consistency —
mindset, motivation, habits, self-love, peace, school, and dreams.

Your future self will thank you.

Reflection:
Where do I want to be more consistent in my life?

____

____

Daily Exercise – Goal in Mini-Steps

Area I want to stay consistent in:

____

Step 1: _______________________

Step 2: _______________________

Step 3: _______________________

DAY 61
CREATE BALANCE INSIDE YOURSELF

Mood Check

Circle how you feel today.

One Word for Today

Write your word for today in the box.

Gratitude
Today I'm thankful for...

DAY 61
MINDSET COACHING

Balance doesn't always mean everything is perfect.
It means you're learning to listen to your needs...
to slow down when you're tired,
to breathe when you're stressed,
to focus when it matters,
and rest when you need to recharge.

Today, bring awareness to the areas of your life that feel heavy — and
the ones that feel light.
Notice what needs more attention and what needs less.

You don't have to balance everything at once.
Just start with one thing.

Reflection:
Where in my life do I need more balance today?

____

____

Daily Exercise – Breathe + Reset
Take 5 slow breaths.

Before breathing, I felt: _______________________________

After breathing, I feel: _______________________________

DAY 62
FIND PEACE IN YOUR OWN PRESENCE

Mood Check

Circle how you feel today.

One Word for Today

Write your word for today in the box.

Gratitude
Today I'm thankful for...

DAY 62
MINDSET COACHING

You spend every moment of your life with yourself — your thoughts, your emotions, your dreams, your hopes, your fears.

Learning to feel comfortable in your own presence is one of the most powerful forms of self-growth.

Today, let yourself be with YOU —
 without judgment, without pressure,
 without comparing yourself to others.

Give yourself kindness.
Give yourself understanding.
Give yourself space to grow.

You deserve peace within yourself.

Reflection:
What helps me feel at peace with myself?

____

____

Daily Exercise – Creative Spark
Draw a symbol or simple image that represents peace to you.
Add one word that matches that symbol:

Word: _______________________________________

WEEK 9 REFLECTION: YOU'RE GROWING QUIETLY AND POWERFULLY

Weekly Wins:

   1. ____

   2. ____

A Challenge I Faced:

____

What I Learned This Week:

____

How I Took Care of My Mindset:

____

One Way I Will Grow Next Week:

____

✦ **Creative Reflection Prompt:**
Write a short journal entry starting with:
"This week, I realized…"

____

____

Creative Space:
Draw or write anything that represents your growth this week.

DAY 64
RELEASE WHAT YOU CAN'T CARRY ANYMORE

Mood Check

Circle how you feel today.

One Word for Today

Write your word for today in the box.

Gratitude
Today I'm thankful for...

I LET GO OF WHAT WEIGHS ME DOWN.

DAY 64
MINDSET COACHING

Sometimes we carry thoughts, emotions, responsibilities, or expectations that are too heavy for our hearts.

You don't have to hold onto everything.
You are allowed to release the things that drain you, stress you, or make you doubt yourself.

Letting go doesn't mean you don't care — it means you're protecting your peace.

Today is a day to lighten your mind,
open your heart,
and give yourself permission to move forward.

Reflection:
What is one thing I'm ready to release today?

____

____

Daily Exercise – Mind Dump → Mind Shift
Mind Dump:

____

Mind Shift :

____

DAY 65
BE THANKFUL FOR HOW FAR YOU'VE COME

Mood Check

Circle how you feel today.

One Word for Today

Write your word for today in the box.

Gratitude
Today I'm thankful for...

DAY 65
MINDSET COACHING

Your journey hasn't been easy — but you're still here.
 Still learning.
 Still growing.
 Still showing up.

Give yourself credit for the steps you've taken,
 the moments you didn't quit,
 the days you pushed through,
 the times you tried again.

Gratitude for your own growth is a form of self-love.

Today, look at yourself with pride.
Recognize the strength it took to get here.

Reflection:
What progress am I grateful for today?

____

____

Daily Exercise – Gratitude 3

1. ____

2. ____

3. ____

Circle the one that means the most today.

DAY 66

REDIRECT YOUR THOUGHTS TOWARD WHAT LIFTS YOU UP

Mood Check

Circle how you feel today.

One Word for Today

Write your word for today in the box.

Gratitude

Today I'm thankful for...

DAY 66
MINDSET COACHING

You won't always control the thoughts that pop into your mind — but you can choose which ones you feed, which ones you focus on, and which ones you let fade away.

Today is about redirecting your thoughts.
When doubt shows up, choose truth.
When negativity appears, choose gratitude.
When fear whispers, choose courage.

This is called mental strength — and you're building it every day.

Reflection:
What thought do I want to redirect today?

____

____

Daily Exercise – Act of Kindness
Do one kind thing today — big or small.

My act of kindness today:
____

How it made me feel:
____

DAY 67
YOU ARE ALLOWED TO TAKE UP SPACE

Mood Check

Circle how you feel today.

One Word for Today

Write your word for today in the box.

Gratitude
Today I'm thankful for...

DAY 67
MINDSET COACHING

You don't have to shrink to make others comfortable.
You don't have to hide your personality, your gifts, your voice, or your potential.

You belong in the spaces you step into —
school, friendships, activities, opportunities, dreams, and goals.
You bring something no one else can bring.

Stand tall today.
Show up as your full self.

Remember that belonging begins within you, not in how others respond.

Reflection:
Where in my life do I need to show up with more confidence?

____

____

Daily Exercise – Goal in Mini-Steps

Big goal I want to work toward: _______________________________

Step 1: ____________________

Step 2: ____________________

Step 3: ____________________

DAY 68
CONFIDENCE STARTS WITH HOW YOU TREAT YOURSELF

Mood Check

Circle how you feel today.

One Word for Today

Write your word for today in the box.

Gratitude
Today I'm thankful for...

DAY 68
MINDSET COACHING

Confidence isn't about being the loudest or the boldest — it starts quietly in how you speak to yourself.

When you say things like...
"I can do this,"
"I am learning,"
"I am valuable,"
"I am growing,"
you build inner strength.

Be your own encourager today.
Speak to yourself like someone who believes in your success.
Because you should — you deserve that kind of support.

Reflection:
What is one confident belief I want to hold about myself?

____

____

Daily Exercise – Breathe + Reset
Take 5 slow breaths.

Before breathing, I felt: _________________________________

After breathing, I feel: _________________________________

DAY 69
CELEBRATE YOUR PROGRESS WITH PRIDE

Mood Check

Circle how you feel today.

One Word for Today

Write your word for today in the box.

Gratitude
Today I'm thankful for...

I AM PROUD OF THE PROGRESS I'M MAKING.

DAY 69
MINDSET COACHING

You've come a long way — in your mindset, your habits, your confidence, your self-awareness, your emotional growth.

Even on the days when it felt hard, you chose to keep going.

Recognize that strength.
Honor it.
Celebrate it.
You deserve to feel proud of the work you're doing —
not just for the big moments,
but for every step forward.

Reflection:
What part of my journey am I most proud of today?

____

____

Daily Exercise – Creative Spark
Draw or doodle something that symbolizes "trust" to you.

Add one word that matches the drawing.
Word: _______________________________________

WEEK 10 REFLECTION: NOTICE THE STRENGTH YOU GAINED

Weekly Wins:
1. ____
2. ____

A Challenge I Faced:
____

What I Learned This Week:
____

How I Took Care of My Mindset:
____

One Way I Will Grow Next Week:
____

Creative Space:
Draw, sketch, write, or express something that represents your week.
This is your space — be real, be creative, be honest.

DAY 71

YOU ARE GROWING INTO SOMEONE STRONGER

Mood Check

Circle how you feel today.

One Word for Today

Write your word for today in the box.

Gratitude
Today I'm thankful for...

EVERY DAY, I AM BECOMING STRONGER.

DAY 71
MINDSET COACHING

Strength doesn't always look like confidence or boldness.

Sometimes strength looks like:
- showing up on a hard day
- trying again after a setback
- saying "no" when something isn't good for you
- asking for help
- keeping your head up
- choosing peace over drama
- believing in yourself, even a little

You have grown in ways you don't always see.
And you continue to grow — in courage, clarity, and emotional strength.

Today, recognize your progress.
It matters.

Reflection:
Where in my life can I see signs of my strength?

____

____

Daily Exercise – Mind Dump → Mind Shift
Mind Dump: _______________________________________

Mind Shift: _______________________________________

DAY 72

YOU ARE MORE CAPABLE THAN YOU THINK

Mood Check

Circle how you feel today.

One Word for Today

Write your word for today in the box.

Gratitude

Today I'm thankful for...

DAY 72
MINDSET COACHING

You may not realize it, but you already have the skills you need to grow into the next version of yourself.

You can learn.
You can adapt.
You can change your habits.
You can shape your mindset.
You can rise to challenges.
You can move forward — step by step.

Today, look at yourself with possibility instead of doubt.
Possibility opens doors.
Doubt closes them.

You are becoming someone powerful, and the work you're doing now is building that future.

Reflection:
What do I want to believe I am capable of?

____

____

Daily Exercise – Gratitude 3
Write 3 things you're grateful for today:

1. _______________________________________

2. _______________________________________

3. _______________________________________

Circle the one that means the most today.

DAY 73
YOUR GROWTH IS BECOMING REAL

Mood Check

Circle how you feel today.

One Word for Today

Write your word for today in the box.

Gratitude
Today I'm thankful for...

MY GROWTH IS REAL, AND I CAN SEE IT IN WHO I'M BECOMING.

DAY 73
MINDSET COACHING

Growth doesn't always show up in big, obvious moments.
Most of the time, it's quiet.

It's in the way you respond instead of react.
It's in the way you think things through.
It's in the way you choose peace, set boundaries, or keep going when things feel hard.

You may not feel different every day—but you are.
The work you've been doing is showing up in your mindset, your choices, and your strength.

Today, take a moment to recognize that.
Not just where you're going—but who you already are becoming.

You're not starting over.
You're evolving.

Reflection:

How can I tell I've grown based on how I think and act now?

____

____

Daily Exercise – Act of Kindness

My act of kindness today: _______________________________________

How it made me feel: ____

DAY 74
BE PROUD OF YOUR JOURNEY, NOT JUST THE OUTCOMES

Mood Check

Circle how you feel today.

One Word for Today

Write your word for today in the box.

Gratitude
Today I'm thankful for...

DAY 74
MINDSET COACHING

We often focus on the final achievement — the grade, the win, the goal, the outcome.
But the journey is where the real growth happens.

Your effort matters.
Your progress matters.
Your attempts matter.
Your learning matters.
Your character development matters.

Be proud of how far you've come — not only where you're going.
Today, take a moment to honor your steps, not just your finish lines.

Reflection:
What part of my journey am I proud of right now?

____

____

Daily Exercise – Goal in Mini-Steps

Big goal I want to work toward: _________________________

Step 1: _____________________

Step 2: _____________________

Step 3: _____________________

DAY 75

YOU BRING LIGHT INTO THE WORLD

Mood Check

Circle how you feel today.

One Word for Today

Write your word for today in the box.

Gratitude

Today I'm thankful for...

DAY 75
MINDSET COACHING

Sometimes you forget how powerful your presence really is.
The way you listen.
The way you care.
The way you speak.
The way you show up.
The way you bring warmth, humor, kindness, or joy into someone's day.

You matter — not because of what you do, but because of who you are.

Today, remember that your light influences others, even in ways you may never know.

Reflection:
What positive impact do I think I make on others?

____

____

Daily Exercise – Breathe + Reset
Take 5 slow breaths.

Before breathing, I felt: _______________________________

After breathing, I feel: _______________________________

DAY 76
BELIEVE IN THE PERSON YOU'RE BECOMING

Mood Check

Circle how you feel today.

One Word for Today

Write your word for today in the box.

Gratitude
Today I'm thankful for...

DAY 76
MINDSET COACHING

Belief is powerful.
It lifts you.
It guides you.
It fuels you.
It shapes the choices you make every single day.

What you believe about yourself becomes the foundation of your future.
So choose beliefs that support your growth —
 not beliefs that limit you.

You don't have to believe in everything all at once.
Just start by believing in your next step.
Your next opportunity.
Your next moment of courage.
You are becoming someone amazing — and your future is something to look forward to.

Reflection:
What is one belief I want to carry into my future?

____

____

Daily Exercise – Creative Spark
Draw or doodle something that symbolizes "trust" to you.

Add one word that matches the drawing.
Word: _______________________________________

WEEK 11 REFLECTION: SEE THE STRENGTH YOU BUILT

Weekly Wins:
  1. ____
  2. ____

A Challenge I Faced:
____

What I Learned This Week:
____

How I Took Care of My Mindset:
____

One Way I Will Grow Next Week:
____

Creative Space:
Draw, sketch, write, or express something that represents your week. This is your space — be real, be creative, be honest.

DAY 78
YOUR EMOTIONS ARE TEACHERS, NOT ENEMIES

Mood Check

Circle how you feel today.

One Word for Today

Write your word for today in the box.

Gratitude
Today I'm thankful for...

DAY 78
MINDSET COACHING

You are not "too emotional."
You are human.

Your emotions — even the uncomfortable ones — are messengers.
They tell you what you need,
what hurts,
what matters,
what feels good,
and what deserves attention.

Instead of fighting your emotions, try listening to them.
 Ask:
 "What is this feeling trying to show me?"
Understanding your emotions is one of the most powerful skills you can
ever develop.

Reflection:
What emotion have I been feeling lately — and what do I think it's telling
me?

____

____

Daily Exercise – Mind Dump → Mind Shift
Mind Dump (emotion or thought weighing on me):

____

Mind Shift (what I can learn or understand from it):

____

DAY 79
YOU ARE WRITING YOUR OWN STORY

Mood Check

Circle how you feel today.

One Word for Today

Write your word for today in the box.

Gratitude
Today I'm thankful for...

DAY 79
MINDSET COACHING

No matter where you started, no matter what challenges you've faced, you are writing your own story — sentence by sentence, day by day.

Your story is not defined by your mistakes.
Your story is not defined by other people.
Your story is not defined by your fears.

It is defined by your choices.
Your courage.
Your growth.
Your dreams.
Your heart.

Today, take a moment to think about the kind of story you want to tell with your life.
This is your chapter.
Your journey.
Your voice.

Reflection:
If my life were a book, what would I want this chapter to be about?

____

____

Daily Exercise – Gratitude 3
Write 3 things you're grateful for today:

1. ____

2. ____

3. ____

Circle the one that means the most today.

DAY 80

YOUR LIGHT AND PURPOSE ARE BECOMING CLEARER

Mood Check

Circle how you feel today.

One Word for Today

Write your word for today in the box.

Gratitude

Today I'm thankful for...

DAY 80
MINDSET COACHING

Purpose doesn't always show up with a big announcement.
It reveals itself slowly —
through what excites you,
what brings you joy,
what you're naturally good at,
and what you feel drawn toward.

Today, listen to the hints your life is giving you.
What do you enjoy?
What activities make you lose track of time?
What makes you feel alive?
These clues matter.

Your purpose is not something you have to rush or force.
It grows as you grow.

Reflection:
What is one thing I feel naturally drawn to or excited about?

____

____

Daily Exercise – Act of Kindness

My act of kindness today: _______________________________

How it made me feel: _________________________________

DAY 81

YOU ARE STEPPING INTO A NEW LEVEL OF CONFIDENCE

Mood Check

Circle how you feel today.

One Word for Today

Write your word for today in the box.

Gratitude

Today I'm thankful for...

DAY 81

MINDSET COACHING

Every time you try again,
every time you speak up,
every time you take a small risk,
every time you choose courage,
you build confidence.

You may not notice the change, but your confidence has been growing throughout this journal journey.

Today, acknowledge that growth.

Believe in the person you're becoming.

Reflection:
Where can I see new confidence in myself?

____

____

Daily Exercise – Goal in Mini-Steps

Big goal I want to work toward: _______________________________

Step 1: _______________________

Step 2: _______________________

Step 3: _______________________

DAY 82
YOUR VOICE MATTERS AND YOUR STORY MATTERS

Mood Check

Circle how you feel today.

One Word for Today

Write your word for today in the box.

Gratitude

Today I'm thankful for...

DAY 82
MINDSET COACHING

Your voice is powerful.
Your perspective is important.
Your experiences matter.

You may not always feel heard or understood, but that doesn't change the truth of your worth.

You have a story —
a real, meaningful story
full of lessons, resilience, growth, and becoming.

Today, allow yourself to feel proud of your story,
even the hard chapters,
because they shaped you into someone strong.

Reflection:
What part of my story am I proud of today?

____

____

Daily Exercise – Breathe + Reset
Take 5 slow breaths.

Before breathing, I felt: ______________________________

After breathing, I feel: ______________________________

DAY 83
CELEBRATE WHO YOU ARE RIGHT NOW

Mood Check

Circle how you feel today.

One Word for Today

Write your word for today in the box.

Gratitude
Today I'm thankful for...

DAY 83
MINDSET COACHING

You've grown so much —
braver, wiser, calmer, kinder, more aware, more grounded.

You don't need to wait until you reach a final goal
to celebrate yourself.

You can celebrate who you are right now:
- your progress,
- your strengths,
- your reflections,
- your self-awareness,
- your dedication to this journey.

Today, look at yourself with admiration.
You deserve to feel proud.

Reflection:
What do I love most about the person I am becoming?

____

____

Daily Exercise – Creative Spark
Design a tiny "book cover" sketch for the chapter you're in right now.
Include a title that represents your life today:

Title: _____________________________________

WEEK 12 REFLECTION: HONOR THE LESSONS OF THIS SEASON

Weekly Wins:
1. ____
2. ____

A Challenge I Faced:
____

What I Learned This Week:
____

How I Took Care of My Mindset:
____

One Way I Will Grow Next Week:
____

Creative Space:
Draw, sketch, write, or express something that represents your week.
This is your space — be real, be creative, be honest.

DAY 85
GROUND YOURSELF BEFORE YOUR NEXT CHAPTER

Mood Check

Circle how you feel today.

One Word for Today

Write your word for today in the box.

Gratitude
Today I'm thankful for...

DAY 85
MINDSET COACHING

Before you step into the final five days, pause and breathe.
Ground yourself.
Center yourself.
Calm your mind.
Connect with your heart.

You've learned so much about yourself.
You've pushed through challenges.
You've discovered strengths you didn't know you had.
You've become more aware, more intentional, more YOU.

Today is a reset — a moment to collect everything you've gained before stepping into your final reflection.

Reflection:
What do I want to bring with me into the last 5 days?

____

____

Daily Exercise – Mind Dump → Mind Shift
Mind Dump (a fear or doubt about being yourself):

____

Mind Shift (the truth that replaces it):

____

____

DAY 86
REFLECT ON THE PERSON YOU'VE BECOME

Mood Check

Circle how you feel today.

One Word for Today

Write your word for today in the box.

Gratitude
Today I'm thankful for...

DAY 86
MINDSET COACHING

You've completed 86 days of showing up, reflecting, growing, stretching, thinking, and understanding yourself more deeply.

Pause and look at yourself with pride.
You're not the same person you were on Day 1 — you're wiser, calmer, more aware, and more connected to who you are.

Growth isn't always loud; sometimes it's quiet and internal.
But it's real.

Today is about honoring your growth and recognizing how far you've come.

Reflection:
What changes do I notice in myself since starting this journal?

____

____

Daily Exercise – Gratitude 3

1. ____

2. ____

3. ____

Circle the one that means the most today.

DAY 87

YOUR STRENGTH HAS CARRIED YOU THROUGH

Mood Check

Circle how you feel today.

One Word for Today

Write your word for today in the box.

Gratitude

Today I'm thankful for...

I AM STRONGER THAN THE CHALLENGES I'VE FACED.

DAY 87
MINDSET COACHING

Think back over these past months — the hard days, the overwhelming moments, the time you didn't feel motivated, and yet... you kept going.

That's strength.
Real strength.
Not the kind people clap for... the quiet kind, inside your heart.

Today is about recognizing that strength and reminding yourself that if you made it through these challenges, you can make it through the ones ahead, too.

Reflection:
What challenge did I overcome that I'm proud of?

____

____

Daily Exercise – Act of Kindness
Do one kind thing today — big or small.

My act of kindness today: ______________________________________

How it made me feel: ____

DAY 88
CELEBRATE YOUR JOURNEY AND YOUR WINS

Mood Check

Circle how you feel today.

One Word for Today

Write your word for today in the box.

Gratitude
Today I'm thankful for...

DAY 88
MINDSET COACHING

You've had big wins, small wins, and invisible wins that only you know about.

All of them matter.

Celebrate the moments you grew.
Celebrate the days you kept going.
Celebrate the times you chose peace.
Celebrate the healing that took place quietly.
Celebrate YOU.

You earned this moment.

Today, let celebration be your mindset.
You've done something powerful — and you deserve to feel proud.

Reflection:
What are 3 things I want to celebrate about myself?

1. ____

2. ____

3. ____

Daily Exercise – Goal in Mini-Steps

Big goal I want to work toward: _______________________________

Step 1: _______________________

Step 2: _______________________

Step 3: _______________________

DAY 89
SET YOUR VISION FOR THE FUTURE

Mood Check

Circle how you feel today.

One Word for Today

Write your word for today in the box.

Gratitude
Today I'm thankful for...

DAY 89
MINDSET COACHING

A new version of you is emerging — one who is more aware, more confident, and more grounded.

Now it's time to dream forward.
Not with pressure... but with excitement.
What do you want to do next?
Who do you want to become?
How do you want to feel?

Your next chapter doesn't have to be perfect — it just has to be yours.

Reflection:
What is one thing I want to focus on in my next chapter?

____

____

Daily Exercise – Vision-Setting
Write one intention for your next season of life:

____

✨ **Creative Reflection Prompt:**
Draw or write a symbol of what your "next chapter" looks like.

DAY 90
YOU DID IT. HONOR THIS MOMENT.

Mood Check

Circle how you feel today.

One Word for Today

Write your word for today in the box.

Gratitude
Today I'm thankful for...

DAY 90
MINDSET COACHING

You've completed 90 days of showing up for yourself.
That is powerful.
That is rare.
That is something you will remember for the rest of your life.

This isn't just the end of a journal — this is the beginning of a stronger, more confident, more grounded YOU.

Today, take a moment of silence for yourself.
For your healing.
For your growth.
For your commitment.
For your courage.

You earned this.

Reflection:
How has this 90-day journey changed me?

____

____

____

Daily Exercise – Closing Letter
On the next page, write a short letter to your future self.
Tell them what you hope for them, what you want them to remember, and what you believe they're capable of.

DEAR FUTURE ME,

FINAL CREATIVE MOMENT

Draw, color, or express anything that symbolizes your journey's completion — a sunrise, a key, a heart, a path, a crown, a flame... anything that feels right.

✨ **YOU COMPLETED 90 DAYS OF GROWTH** ✨

You showed up.
You stayed committed.
You worked on your mindset.
You learned yourself.
You pushed through the hard days and celebrated the good ones.

That takes strength.
That takes courage.
That takes HEART.

BE PROUD OF WHO YOU ARE.

BE EXCITED FOR WHO YOU'RE BECOMING.

This isn't goodbye — this is your launch into the next version of YOU.

Keep growing.
Keep believing.
Keep shining.
The world needs your light.
And you're just getting started.

With pride and belief in you,

Dr. Shamarah J. Hutchins

TheMindologist

Stay In Touch!

Your Journey is just beginning,
and we're here to support!

🌐 www.themindologistdoc.com

📷 @themindologist

🧵 themindologist